Table Of Contents

Easy Veggie P...

Welcome To Easy Veggie Pasta Recipes
Pasta Is Made From Many Different Types of Grains
    Egg Noodles or Egg Pasta:
    Kamut Pasta:
    Semolina Pasta:
    Spelt Pasta:
    Whole Wheat Pasta:
    Gluten Free Pastas:
    Alternative Grain Pastas:
        Amaranth Pasta:
        Brown Rice Pasta:
        Buckwheat
        Corn
        Green Banana Pasta
        Millet Pasta:
        Organic Pasta:
        Quinoa Pasta:
        Rice Pasta:
Easy Veggie Pasta Recipes
    Spaghetti with Garlic & Oil
    Herbed Garlic Bread
    Orecchiette with Broccoli Rabe
    Fresh Tomato Basil Sauce with Tortigioni
    The Easiest Pasta and Beans Recipe Ever
    "Egg" Noodles with Italian-Style Savoy Cabbage and Tomatoes
    How to Buy and Store Asparagus
    Lemon Broccoli or Asparagus with Bow Tie Pasta and Gremolata

- Gremolata
- Pasta Shells with Mushrooms and Gremolata
- Rotini with Butternut Squash and Sage
- Bow Tie Pasta with Roasted Cauliflower and Spanish Olives
- Pasta, Beans & Greens
- Bow Tie Pasta with Broccoli, Portabellas & Roasted Peppers
- Skillet Mushroom Stroganoff
- Vegan Sour Cream
- Linguine with Basil & Tomatoes
- How To Roast Garlic
- How to Chiffonade Basil & Other Greens
- Ziti with Eggplant and Tomatoes
- Penne with Mushroom Sauce
- Marinara Sauce
- Vegan Mushroom and Eggplant "Meatballs"

3 Asian Inspired Pasta Dishes
- Hoisin Noodles
- Super Easy Asian Noodles
- Asian Style Noodles With Tofu & Vegetables

Thanks For Your Purchase

Check Out My Other Books Available on amazon Kindle:
- How To Transition To A Vegan or Vegetarian Lifestyle
- Stocking The Vegan or Vegetarian Pantry
- Easy Veggie Burgers
- Easy Veggie Soups
- Easy Vegetarian Cooking With Herbs
- Hazels Pickles

Welcome To Easy Veggie Pasta Recipes

Whichever variety you choose, pasta dishes can be quick to cook, delicious to eat, and nutritious. Pasta is also a great choice when creating economical dishes or feeding a crowd. Pasta pairs nicely with almost any flavors and is a perfect way to showcase vegetables at their peak of freshness. Pasta dresses up nicely for company or happily dresses down for a family dinner. It's kid friendly too! What more could you ask for? Let's begin by taking a short look at the different ingredients you'll find pasta made from:

Pasta Is Made From Many Different Types of Grains

Egg Noodles or Egg Pasta

Egg pasta has a yellowish color but it isn't always made with eggs. You have to read the label to determine if they contain eggs or not as looks can be deceiving. When egg noodles are actually made with egg, they use only the yolk. Semolina flour is a coarser, durable flour and it will bind better than all-purpose flour which is fine and delicate.

Kamut Pasta

Kamut™ is the registered product name for the wheat variety Q-77 or Khorasan wheat which is a species of wheat that produces grains twice the size of common wheat. It's thought that some people with wheat sensitivity can tolerate Kamut™ but it's completely off limits to people who suffer from celiac disease. Pasta is made from the whole grain wheat Kamut™. This grain has a natural nutty, buttery flavor. Protein values for Kamut™ are twenty to forty percent higher than "normal" wheat giving an added benefit along with it's delicious flavor. It also contains higher values of amino acids, lipids, vitamins and minerals. Kamut™ is also easier to digest. Kamut™ is mostly grown by farmers in the fields of Africa with lots of pride and without the use of any chemicals or pesticides. All pasta made with Kamut™ is organic pasta because it is never hybridized for genetic modification. Kamut™ is a registered trademark.

Semolina Pasta

Semolina is the type of flour that is most commonly used to make pasta. Semolina comes from Durum wheat which is Winter wheat and is considered the best wheat to use when making pasta. The best quality durum wheat in the world is found in Italy. Semolina has a more yellowish color than wheat used to make standard all-purpose flour.

Spelt Pasta

Spelt is a whole grain that has a similar flavor and texture to wheat. Spelt does contain gluten, so people with gluten sensitivity should not use spelt as a substitute for wheat. Spelt is an ancient grain which is a relative to wheat. It has a nutty flavor, a broader span of nutrients than wheat, and is an excellent source of vitamin B2, copper, niacin, manganese, and thiamin.

Whole Wheat Pasta

Whole Wheat pasta is made in the same way as semolina pasta but the hulls of the wheat are retained when the wheat is milled. This gives the pasta a darker color and a richer wheaty, nutty flavor.

Gluten Free Pastas

Gluten is the key ingredient which gives pasta its flavor. Given that wheat is the primary ingredient in pasta, it contains a lot of gluten. If you're on a gluten free diet, regular pasta is off limits to you. The good news is that there are now gluten free pastas available in the marketplace. These are generally made from ingredients such as buckwheat, corn, rice, brown rice, quinoa and others such as spelt and amaranth.

Alternative Grain Pastas

There are several alternative grains which have come to be commonly used as alternatives to semolina in the pasta making process. Here's a list of some of the alternate ingredients:

Amaranth Pasta

People who are able to tolerate spinach and beets well may also be able to tolerate the highly nutritious seeds, leaves, and flour of amaranth. Amaranth has a nutty, pleasant flavor. In addition to being used in pasta making, it also makes great bagels, bread, cookies, doughnuts gravies, muffins, pancakes, and sauces, as well as many other things. Amaranth pasta is gluten free, light brown in color; and when cooked, is the color of whole-wheat noodles and has the consistency of semolina pasta.

Brown Rice Pasta

Brown Rice pasta is made with brown rice and is also gluten free, wheat free and usually naturally low in sodium. Chances are you won't find brown rice pasta in a Asian market as this type of pasta is found almost exclusively in health food stores.

Buckwheat

Soba is a type of thin noodle made from buckwheat. In Japan, soba can be used to refer to any thin noodle Soba noodles are served either hot or cold. If cold,
they're served with a dipping sauce, and if hot, they're served in a broth as a noodle soup. Thick noodles in Japan are known as Udon and made from wheat.

Corn

Corn pasta is pasta that is made from ground corn. Usually it is offered as a gluten-free alternative to semolina pasta for people with gluten intolerance. There are others who eat corn pasta simply because they enjoy the texture and flavor. Corn pasta is usually found in the gluten free section of major grocery stores as well as smaller health food stores if you have a gluten intolerance, its best, as with any product, to read packages thoroughly to ensure you are purchasing a gluten-free product. Corn pasta is made in much the same way as traditional semolina pasta. It's made by grinding corn into flour, kneading together with water, and rolling the dough out or forcing it through pasta disks to make shapes. Corn pasta is available in a variety of shapes, including flat pastas such as linguine and others such as corn elbows. Corn pasta is often flavored with ingredients such as spinach, peppers, and sundried tomatoes. Depending on the variety of corn used the color of corn pasta ranges from creamy white to yellow in color. Sometimes food coloring is added to make pasta yellow, because people associate corn with the color yellow.

Green Banana Pasta

Excerpted from Science Daily (June 22, 2012) — "People with celiac disease struggle with limited food choices, as their condition makes them unable to tolerate gluten, found in wheat and other grains. Researchers from the University of Brazil have developed a gluten-free pasta product from green banana flour, which tasters found more acceptable than regular whole wheat pasta. The product has less fat and is cheaper to produce than standard pastas."source

Millet Pasta

The first historically recorded pasta in history was made by the

Chinese 7,000 years ago. The grain they used to make their pasta was millet. While today it's considered an alternative grain, millet was actually the first to be used in pasta making. Millet is gluten-free and also a good source of B vitamins particularly niacin and B6. Again, I caution you to read labels, as sometimes. These "alternative" pastas can contain a mixture of wheat and other grains.

Organic Pasta

Most of the pasta which comes from Italy is organic. Preservatives aren't necessary in the process of making pasta, however, to be considered as organic in the U.S., it has to be certified organic to be sold as organic so that makes labeling imported pasta as organic impossible.

Quinoa Pasta

The Incas called it Quinoa, the mother grain. It's a tiny, gluten free seed, not a grain that was first grown
by the Incas in the Andean regions of Colombia, Peru, Ecuador and Bolivia 3000 to 4000 years ago. Quinoa is not only gluten free; it's also cholesterol free, and very low in sodium. Quinoa is the only complete protein grain and supplies all the essential amino acids. Quinoa is often combined with corn flour to create delicious, nutritionally dense pasta.

Rice Pasta

Rice Pastas are naturally gluten free and are typically found typically found in Asian specialty food markets. Today it's also possible to find mainstream pasta brands offering this type of pasta as a gluten free alternative and marketed as Italian pasta.

Easy Veggie Pasta Recipes

All of these recipes take less than an hour to cook which makes them great for those busy weeknight dinners.

Spaghetti with Garlic & Oil

This dish is SO easy it almost cooks itself. I must admit, when making this for myself, I easily double the amount of crushed red pepper I've specified. One of the nice things about it is its earthy. uncomplicated, simplicity. It's also very open to tossing whatever veggies you might have on hand into the sauté pan along with the garlic. However; in its pure form it'll soon become a favored comfort food. Serve this simply. Add some tossed salad greens & a loaf of garlic bread. Try the garlic bread recipe that follows! This is an especially delicious late night food to indulge in after a night out. Enjoy!

You'll Need:
Kosher salt for cooking pasta plus 1 teaspoon
1 pound thin spaghetti
5-6 cloves garlic, minced
1/2 cup extra-virgin olive oil
1/2 teaspoon red pepper flakes
1/4 cup flat-leaf parsley, finely minced
1 lemon, zested
Juice 1 lemon
Freshly ground black pepper, to taste
Freshly grated Parmigiano-Reggiano, optional

Directions:
Place a large pot of water on the stove over high heat, bring to a boil,

add a generous amount of salt. Allow water to return to a boil, add pasta.

Cook, stirring occasionally, about 8-10 minutes until pasta is cooked al dente and not soft.

Drain in a colander, reserving about 1/4 cup of cooking water.

Meanwhile, while pasta cooks, in a large skillet over low heat, heat olive oil, add garlic, 1 teaspoon salt and crushed red pepper flakes. Cook, stirring occasionally, about 8 minutes or until the garlic becomes soft and golden.

Add the pasta and 1/4 cup reserved pasta cooking water to the skillet. Mix well.

Add the parsley, lemon zest, lemon juice and freshly ground black pepper. Adjust seasoning, to taste.

Transfer to a large serving bowl or divide into 4 to 6 pasta bowls. Serve topped with grated Parmigiano-Reggiano cheese, if desired.

Variation: Substitute 1 large bunch of fresh basil, minced, for the parsley. Prep Time: 10 minutes
Cook Time: 18 minutes
Total Time: 28 minutes
Yield: 4 to 6 servings
Difficulty Level: Easy

Herbed Garlic Bread

You'll Need:
4 tablespoons butter or vegan butter, room temperature
2 cloves garlic, finely minced
1/2 teaspoon fresh ground black pepper
2 tablespoons fresh basil
1 tablespoon fresh flat leaf parsley, minced
1 tablespoon fresh oregano, minced
1 loaf French bread, cut into 1/2" slices

Directions:
Preheat oven to 350° F.

In a small bowl, beat butter, garlic, basil, pepper, parsley, & oregano together until light and fluffy.

Spread butter mixture over one cut side of bread, laying it on an ungreased baking sheet as you go.

Bake at 350° F. for 10-15 minutes or until butter is melted and edges of bread are slightly browned.

Serve immediately.

Variation: Substitute other fresh herbs you might have on hand such as chives, rosemary, thyme or tarragon.

Cook Time: 15 minutes
Total Time 20 minutes
Yield: 8-10 slices
Difficulty: Easy

Orecchiette with Broccoli Rabe

Broccoli Rabe is also known as rapini, broccoletti, cime di rapa, rapé, rappi, raap, raab, and friarielli. Broccoli rabe is a leafy, green vegetable with small clusters of green buds which resemble broccoli. It's flavor is nutty, bitter, and pungent.

Broccoli Rabe has a unique, delicious flavor which can't be duplicated but if unavailable, you can substitute kale, spinach or Swiss chard in this recipe. Other substitutes are thinly sliced or shredded Brussel sprouts or frozen Lima beans. Add a little thyme if using Limas! They're outstanding choices!

You'll Need:
1 pound orecchiette
1 (1-lb) bunch broccoli rabe, washed well, hollow stems removed, and leaves and remaining stems cut into 2-inch pieces
1 cup (or more) vegetable broth
5 tablespoons extra virgin olive oil, divided
5 garlic cloves, finely chopped
1/2 to 3/4 teaspoon dried hot red-pepper flakes (to taste)
3/4 teaspoon salt
 Freshly ground black pepper
1 teaspoon (or more to taste) Sherry wine vinegar
Optional: 2 ounces pine nuts 2 ounces sun dried tomatoes (packed in oil), roughly chopped Accompaniment: grated parmesan

Directions:
Cook pasta according to package instructions until pasta is al dente Drain in a colander and transfer to a large serving bowl.
 Heat 4 tablespoons oil in large nonstick skillet over medium heat. Add garlic and dried crushed pepper; stir until garlic is pale golden, about 1 minute. Add greens by large handfuls; stir just until beginning to wilt before adding more, tossing with tongs to coat with oil. Add 1 cup broth, cover, and simmer until greens are just tender, adding more

broth by tablespoonful if dry, 1 to 10 minutes.

Add optional sun dried tomatoes and/or pine nuts.

Simmer uncovered until heated through and liquid is almost absorbed, about 2 minutes.

Stir in 1 teaspoon vinegar. Season with salt and pepper, And more vinegar if desired; drizzle with remaining 1 tablespoon oil and serve.

Prep Time: 15 minutes
Cook Time: 30 minutes
Total Time: 30 minutes
Yield: 4 to 6 servings
Difficulty Level: Easy

Fresh Tomato Basil Sauce with Tortiglioni

This is the recipe pictured on the cover and a delicious raw tomato sauce. The only "cooking" involved is allowing the sauce to sit so flavors have time to blend. Use the freshest, vine ripened tomatoes you can find! Mangia!

You'll need:
5 large farm fresh, garden ripe tomatoes
1 cup fresh chopped basil leaves
1/2 cup Extra Virgin olive oil
2 cloves garlic, crushed
Kosher salt and freshly ground black pepper, to taste
1 (1 pound box) tortiglioni, or other tubular shaped pasta
Parmesan cheese for garnish (optional)

Directions:
Bring a saucepan full of water to a boil. Spear tomatoes with a fork, one at a time, through the blossom end. Submerge tomato in boiling water for 10 seconds, remove to a bowl and repeat with remaining tomatoes.
Peel tomatoes, cut in half, squeeze out the seeds and dice tomatoes, being careful to catch juice in a bowl. Strain juice to remove seeds.
Chop basil leaves finely.
Mince garlic.
Combine tomatoes, basil, olive oil, garlic, salt and pepper in a glass or ceramic bowl.
Cover and let stand for 1 hour at room temperature.
Cook tortigioni according to package directions.
Combine fresh sauce with hot pasta.
Serve with Parmesan cheese on the side, if desired.

Prep Time: about 15 minutes plus additional time for sauce to sit.
Cook Time: 15 minutes
Total Time: 1 hour 15 minutes

Yield: 4 - 6 servings

The Easiest Pasta and Beans Recipe Ever

Ditalini pasta is also known as small thimbles. It's short, small, tubular pasta which cooks in a hurry. You can easily add a thawed package of cut spinach to this recipe for more color and variety. Add it right along with your tomatoes and garbanzos. Mix things up a bit by using a different kind of canned bean or use two different types at the same time!

You'll Need:
2 Tablespoons olive oil
2 cloves garlic, minced
2 (15 ounce) cans garbanzo beans (DO NOT DRAIN)
1 (14 ounce) can diced tomatoes, drained
1/2 teaspoon thyme
1/2 teaspoon rosemary
1/2 teaspoon oregano
1/2 teaspoon basil
1/2 teaspoon marjoram
1 teaspoons kosher salt
1/4 teaspoons freshly ground black pepper
1 cup ditalini (uncooked)

Directions:
Heat the oil in a 3-4 quart saucepan. Add the garlic and allow to brown slightly. Add the garbanzo beans and their liquid, tomatoes, pasta, herbs, salt, and pepper.
 Bring to a boil, add ditalini and simmer for 15 minutes, stirring occasionally.
 Season to taste and serve. Grate some Parmigiano-Reggiano over each serving
or sprinkle with nutritional yeast flakes.

 Prep Time: 5 minutes
Cook Time: 15 minutes

Total Time: 20 minutes
Yield: 4 servings
Difficulty Level: Easy

"Egg" Noodles with Italian-Style Savoy Cabbage and Tomatoes

Savoy cabbage is a curly, lacy light green cabbage named for the Savoy region, a medieval duchy on the border of Italy, France and Switzerland where it's known as cavolo verza.

Savoy cabbage is the prettiest of all cabbage. It has fantastic crinkly leaves and a contrasting dark on pale color palette. Only a few outer leaves are dark green and the inside is creamy and pale.

Savoy cabbage is very tender, sweet, cooks quickly and easily and lacks the sulfur odor so distinctive in other cabbage varieties. Just don't overcook it.

You'll Need:
1 (12 ounce) package broad "egg" noodles
3 tablespoons extra virgin olive oil
1 large onion, halved and thinly sliced
2 large garlic cloves, minced
1 pound savoy cabbage, cored and thinly sliced (about 4 cups)
2 carrots, peeled and diced
1 (15 ounce) can diced tomatoes in juice, undrained
2 tablespoons red-wine vinegar
1 teaspoon dried thyme
1 Bay leaf
kosher salt, to taste
freshly ground black pepper, to taste
1 tablespoon butter or vegan butter
Optional garnish: Pecorino Romano or nutritional yeast flakes

Directions:
Bring a pot of salted water to a boil and cook "egg" noodles according to package instructions. Meanwhile: You should have about 4 firmly packed cups of cabbage strips.

Place the olive oil in a large sauté pan or Dutch oven over high heat. Add the onion, and sauté until they start to soften and brown. Add the cabbage, carrots and garlic, stirring to blend well.
 Sauté for 5 minutes, stirring occasionally.
Add the tomatoes with juice, vinegar, thyme and bay leaf. Season well with salt and lots of freshly ground black pepper.
 Bring mixture to a boil, reduce heat, and cook, covered, for 30 minutes, or until cabbage is softened and flavors are blended. When ready to serve, stir butter into the cabbage.
Transfer to a serving bowl and pass Pecorino Romano or nutritional yeast flakes separately. Prep Time: 15 minutes
Cook Time: 35 minutes
Total Time: 50 minutes
Yield: 4 servings
Difficulty: Easy

How to Buy and Store Asparagus

Fresh asparagus can be substituted for the broccoli using the same cooking technique. Just about any vegetable you can think of will work in this recipe. Asparagus are very easy to prepare. Just take the band off the bunch and give them a good rinse under cold water. Grasp the spears by the ends and bend them until the end snaps off. Either discard the bottom ends or save them to make vegetable stock. Don't expect them to all break at the same length. They will break where the tough, woody ends are. When you buy asparagus, choose bright green spears with tightly closed buds. Make sure they aren't dried out and try to choose the ones that have damp stem ends.
When you get them home, stand them in a container with a couple of inches of water and they'll store this way in your fridge for nearly a week. The first asparagus of spring are thick, meaty and can be almost as large as your thumb. As the season progresses and the plants get tired, the stalks will become pencil thin. Thicker asparagus will have a meatier texture and a more robust flavor than the thin ones but they're all delicious.
You can add just about anything you have on hand to the sauté pan as the garlic is cooking in this recipe. Thin strips of red bell peppers, mushrooms, cooked carrots or a can of artichoke hearts will go nicely with broccoli. For a heartier dish, add cubed tofu or tempeh to your sauté pan along with your garlic.

Lemon Broccoli or Asparagus with Bow Tie Pasta and Gremolata

You'll Need:
1/4 cup extra virgin olive oil

3 cloves garlic, minced
3 tablespoons freshly squeezed lemon juice
1/2 teaspoon salt
1/8 teaspoon freshly ground black pepper
8 ounces bow tie pasta
1 bunch (about 3 heads) broccoli, cut into florets OR 1 1/2 pounds fresh asparagus, cut into 1 1/2" pieces

Directions:
Prepare Gremolata (recipe follows)
Bring a large pot of salted water to a boil and add pasta.
Cook pasta as directed on package.
About 5 minutes before pasta is done, add broccoli to cooking pasta. Continue to cook until pasta is cooked and broccoli is tender crisp. Drain.
Meanwhile: In a large sauté pan, warm olive oil over low heat. Add garlic and cook slowly until golden, about 2 to 3 minutes, being careful not to burn it.
When pasta and broccoli are cooked, add to sauté pan and toss to thoroughly combine.
Stir in lemon juice, and season with salt and pepper.
Transfer to a large serving bowl.
Sprinkle with Gremolata.

Prep Time: 10 minutes
Cook Time: 15 minutes
Total Time: 25 minutes
Yield: 4 servings
Difficulty: Easy

Gremolata

Gremolata adds freshness to almost any dish. You change it up a bit by substituting orange zest for lemon zest (or not) and oregano or basil for the parsley (or not). It's great on everything from a pizza and pasta to grilled vegetables and soups. You can add it to yogurt for a great veggie dip. Add a couple drops of olive oil keep it moist if you're going to store it for a few days. You can add extra virgin olive oil to it and use it as a substitute for the Argentinean Chimichurri if you're not a fan of cilantro. It makes a nice addition to braised dishes as it lends a zesty freshness to winter menus.

I'm not a kitchen gadget person as a rule. I'm happy with high quality, basic kitchen essentials with only a couple of exceptions. One of those exceptions is an old fashioned, hand held zester. It's a small tool that's capable of making long, fine threads of citrus zest. Personally, this is what I prefer in my Gremolata and on any pasta dish that calls for lemon zest. I've written this assuming you don't own one. Zesters are cheap, less than 10 bucks but they add so much character and freshness to cooking.

When peeling citrus you need to remember to remove only the thin colored layer on the very outside of the fruit. Leave the white pith on the fruit because other than being very bitter, it lacks flavor and will ruin your dish,

You'll Need:
1 lemon
1/4 cup finely chopped fresh flat leaf parsley
3 garlic cloves, finely minced

Directions:
Wash and scrub lemons using cold water and a scrub brush. Wash parsley, dry in paper towels.
Using vegetable peeler, remove peel in long strips from lemon. Mince lemon peel.

Transfer to small bowl
Mix in parsley and garlic.
Can be made 6 hours in advance.
Cover and refrigerate.

Pasta Shells with Mushrooms and Gremolata

Use a variety of fresh mushrooms in this recipe for a deeper, richer flavor.

You'll Need:
1 recipe Gremolata (recipe above)
1 (8 ounce) package medium pasta shells, fiori, rotelle or radiatori pasta
2 tablespoons extra virgin olive oil
2 cloves garlic, finely chopped
1 pound cultivated or wild mushrooms, such as cremini, shiitakes, chanterelles or oyster mushrooms, or a combination, trimmed and quartered if small, cut in thick slices if large
2 tablespoons dry white wine or dry vermouth
salt and freshly ground black pepper to taste
1 tablespoon butter or vegan butter

Directions:
Bring a large pot of lightly salted water to a boil.
 Place the pasta shells in the pot, cook for 8 to 10 minutes, until al dente, and drain.
 Heat the oil in a large skillet over medium heat, and cook the garlic and mushrooms until mushrooms are browned.
Add salt and wine continue to cook, stirring the mushrooms in the pan, until the wine has just about evaporated and the mushrooms are glazed, about 5 minutes, mix in the butter or vegan butter and season with freshly ground black pepper.
 In a large bowl, toss the cooked pasta and the mushroom mixture together.
Serve with Gremolata at the table.

 Prep Time: 15 minutes
 Cook Time: 20 minutes
Total Time: 35 minutes

Yield: 3-4 servings
Difficulty Level: Easy

Rotini with Butternut Squash and Sage

If you look in the produce section of your market, often you'll find pre peeled squash. Any winter squash is suitable for this dish with the exception of blue Hubbard.

I also make this dish using sweet potatoes but you can roast many other vegetables along with the squash. Red bell peppers are especially good as are wedges of onion.

Squash can be difficult to peel but if you cut it into pieces before peeling the job becomes easier. Another way to make the task easier is to score the skin of the squash in a couple of places, microwave it (6 minutes on high power is enough for a 2-pound squash), let it sit for a few minutes then slice it in quarters and peel!

To add protein to this dish add a 10 ounce package of baby lima beans to your cooking pasta during the last 10 minutes of cooking and a little thyme to the shallots or add a 15 ounce can of drained garbanzo beans to the sautéing shallots.

You'll Need:
1 medium Butternut squash
1/4 cup plus 1 tablespoon olive oil
1/2 pound rotini pasta
1/2 teaspoon kosher salt
1/2 teaspoon freshly ground black pepper
2 tablespoons unsalted butter or vegan butter
1/2 cup shallots, finely minced
2 cloves garlic, finely minced
1 tablespoon fresh sage leaves, minced
1/4 cup chopped pecans

Optional garnishes: Parmesan Cheese Pecan halves

Directions:
Peel squash cut into 1/2 inch cubes. You should have about 8 cups of

cubes.
Preheat oven to 400 F.
Toss squash with 1 tablespoon olive oil.
Spread on cookie sheet and sprinkle with salt and pepper.
Bake, stirring every 10 minutes until slightly caramelized, 30 minutes total.
Remove from oven and set aside.
Meanwhile, as squash cooks, cook pasta in boiling water until al dente, drain well, and transfer to serving bowl.
Melt butter with 1/4c olive oil in large sauté pan over medium high heat until it bubbles.
Reduce heat to medium low, add shallot, sage salt and pepper. Cook stirring until shallots are soft (2-3 minutes).
Turn off heat; add the pasta, squash and pecans.
Toss until well combined.
Serve immediately topped with garnishes, if desired.

Prep Time: 15 minutes
Cook Time: 35 minutes
Total Time: 50 minutes
Yield: 4 servings
Difficulty: Easy

Bow Tie Pasta with Roasted Cauliflower and Spanish Olives

The most commonly available Spanish olives are the green ones that come in jars and stuffed with pimentos. You'll want to use pitted, Queen Size olives in this recipe, if possible. If they aren't available, use stuffed Queen olives; the pimentos will add extra color to your dish and won't upset the balance of flavors!

You'll Need:
2 tablespoons butter or vegan butter
2 tablespoons extra virgin olive oil
2 medium shallots, peeled and sliced
1 cauliflower, trimmed and cut into small florets
1/3 cup sliced Spanish olives
1/8 teaspoon salt
1/2 teaspoon crushed red pepper flakes
5 cloves garlic, crushed
12 ounces uncooked bow tie pasta
3 tablespoons fresh parsley, coarsely chopped

Optional garnish: 1 ounce Pecorino Romano cheese, shaved

Directions:
Preheat oven to 450°F.
 Place a small heavy roasting pan in oven and heat until hot. Remove pan from oven. Add butter and oil and swirl to coat. Add shallots and cauliflower to pan and toss to coat. Bake 450°F. for 10 minutes.
 Add olives, salt, crushed red pepper flakes, and garlic. Stir to combine. Return pan to oven and bake 7 - 10 minutes or until cauliflower is tender and brown around the edges.
Bring a pot of water to a boil and cook bow ties 7 minutes, or until almost tender.
Drain pasta over a bowl, reserving 1/2 cup pasta cooking liquid.

Return pasta to pan over medium-high heat.
Add reserved pasta cooking liquid and roasted cauliflower mixture.
Cook, stirring occasionally for 2 minutes or until pasta is al dente.
Remove from heat and stir in parsley.
Garnish with shaved cheese, if desired.

Prep Time: 10 minutes
Cook Time: 25 minutes
Total Time: 35 minutes
Yield: 4 servings Difficulty: Easy

Pasta, Beans & Greens

I like to use medium pasta shells for pasta dishes that contain beans because I find it amusing that the beans always hide in the shells. I know, I'm weird!

You'll Need:
3 tablespoons extra-virgin olive oil
1 carrot, peeled & diced
1 cup onion, chopped
2 cloves garlic, minced
1/4 teaspoon crushed red pepper
2 (15 ounce) cans diced tomatoes, undrained
4 cups vegetable stock
1/2 teaspoon dried oregano
1/2 teaspoon Kosher salt
!/2 teaspoon freshly ground black pepper
1 (15 ounce) can cannellini beans, rinsed & drained
1/2 teaspoon salt, or to taste
Freshly ground pepper, to taste
8 ounces medium pasta shells, uncooked
1 (10 ounce) package frozen, chopped spinach, defrosted

Optional garnish: 1/4 cup freshly grated Parmesan or Pecorino Romano, or Nutritional yeast flakes

Directions:
Place a large pot of water over high heat. Bring to a boil, add a generous amount of salt, and allow to return to a boil. When boiling, add pasta, and cook, stirring occasionally.
Meanwhile, heat oil in a large skillet over low heat; add carrot, onion, garlic, crushed red pepper, salt and pepper. Cook, stirring, until vegetables are soft but not browned, about 4 minutes.
Add tomatoes, stock, and oregano. Cover, increase heat to medium. Cook, stirring occasionally, for 15-20 minutes.

Add beans and spinach, cover, reduce heat to low and simmer an additional 15 minutes.
Add seasoning to taste.
Meanwhile, cook pasta according to package instructions.
Drain in a colander and return to the cooking pot.
Add the tomato mixture, toss to coat.
The dish should be slightly soupy.
Sprinkle each serving with cheese, if desired.

Prep Time: 10 minutes
Cook Time: 40 minutes
Total Time: 50 minutes
Yield: 6-8 servings
Difficulty: Easy

Bow Tie Pasta with Broccoli, Portabellas & Roasted Peppers

You'll Need:
4 cups broccoli florets (from 2 heads)
1 pound bow tie pasta
2 Portabella mushroom caps, wiped clean, stems removed, cut in half and sliced
3 tablespoons extra virgin olive oil
3 cloves garlic, minced
Zest 1 lemon
1/4 teaspoon freshly ground black pepper
1/4 teaspoon cayenne pepper
1 tablespoon fresh lemon juice
1 cup roasted red bell peppers, thinly sliced
2 tablespoons capers

Optional Garnish Freshly grated Parmigiano-Reggiano cheese or Nutritional yeast flakes

Directions:
 Bring a large pot of salted water to a boil, add broccoli florets, cook for 3 minutes. Scoop the broccoli out and transfer to a large serving bowl, reserving water. Allow the water to return to a boil. Add the bow ties and cook about 10 to 12 minutes. Drain well and add to the broccoli. Meanwhile:
Heat olive oil in a large skillet over medium low heat. Add garlic and cook, stirring, for 30 seconds. Add mushrooms and sauté until they lose their raw look.
Add white wine to pan and cook for 2-3 minutes to allow alcohol to burn off.
Add tomato puree and cook for 5 minutes.
Add roasted peppers and cook until heated through. Reduce heat to low, add lemon juice, lemon zest, salt and pepper. Stir to combine.

Add broccoli, bow ties and capers to the pan and heat until heated through. Season mixture to taste.

Pass Parmigiano-Reggiano at the table or nutritional yeast flakes, if desired.

Prep Time: 20 minutes
 Cook Time: 20 minutes
Total Time: 40 minutes
Yield: 4-6 servings
Difficultly: Easy

Skillet Mushroom Stroganoff

This is probably the most creative dish my Mother made when I was a little kid. It's fast, easy, inexpensive & delicious! Use as many different types of mushrooms as you have available for the most flavor or you can substitute crumbles for up to half the mushrooms.

You'll Need:
1/4 cup butter or vegan butter
1 tablespoon vegetable oil
1/2 cup scallions, chopped
2 cloves garlic, minced
1-1/2 pounds assorted fresh mushrooms, (portabella, golden chanterelle, shiitake, cremini, oyster, porcini, etc.) trimmed & some sliced & some chopped
3 tablespoons lemon juice
3 tablespoons burgundy or other dry red wine
1 1/4 cups vegetable stock
1/2 teaspoon Kosher salt
1/4 teaspoon freshly ground black pepper
4 ounces egg noodles, uncooked
1 cup sour cream or vegan sour cream (see recipe below)
fresh scallions. finely chopped fresh flat leaf parsley, finely chopped, optional

Directions:
In a large skillet, melt butter or vegan butter and vegetable oil together.
Add scallions, garlic and mushrooms, sauté until mushrooms are lightly browned.
Stir.in lemon juice, burgundy vegetable stock, salt and pepper.
Bring mixture to a boil, reduce heat and simmer, uncovered, for 15 minutes.
Stir in egg noodles.

Cover and cook 5 minutes.
Remove cover, mix in sour cream or vegan sour cream.
Heat through, being careful not to boil.
Garnish with chopped scallion and fresh parsley, if desired.

Prep Time: 15 minutes
Cook Time: 25 minutes
Total Time: 40 minutes
Yield: 4-6 servings
Difficulty: Easy

Vegan Sour Cream

Vegan Sour Cream recipes can be found all over the Internet. Some work. Some don't. This one works so rather than taking the time to write out my own, which is exactly like this, here's the same recipe from food.com

Vegan Sour Cream Recipe

Two things to note about this recipe. It doesn't freeze as freezing changed the texture of tofu. Also, if you choose to use olive oil instead of canola oil. Use a light olive oil, not extra virgin as it will overpower the other flavors.

This recipe yields about 1 1/2 cups making more than you need for the above recipe.

You'll Need:

1 (16 ounce) package silken tofu
1 tablespoon olive oil (canola oil ok too)
4 -5 teaspoons lemon juice
2 teaspoons apple cider vinegar
1 teaspoon sugar (or your favorite sweetener)
1/2-1 teaspoon salt, to taste

Directions:

Place all ingredients in a blender. Process five minutes, until very creamy and smooth. Refrigerate for at least an hour to thicken. Use within 5-6 days.

Prep Time: 5 minutes
Cook Time: 0
Total Time: 5 minutes
Yield: 1 1/2 cups
Difficulty Level: Easy

Linguine with Basil & Tomatoes

Years ago I owned a restaurant. We had several Vegetarian options on the menu. This was by far the best seller! This may seem like an overwhelming amount of garlic but the process of roasting garlic causes it to develop a sweet, mellow flavor.

You'll Need:
12 ounces linguine
2 heads garlic. roasted (see directions below)
2 tablespoons extra virgin olive oil
1 tablespoon shallots, minced
2 cloves raw garlic, minced
1/4 teaspoon crushed red pepper (or to taste)
1 1/2 teaspoons marjoram
1/2 teaspoon Kosher salt
1 cup dry white wine
2 (15 ounce) cans diced tomatoes in juice
2 tablespoons lemon juice
2 tablespoons butter or vegan butter
1 bunch fresh basil, cut in chiffonade (see directions below)
 freshly ground black pepper, to taste
Zest 1 lemon

Directions:
Roast garlic according to directions below.
Bring a large pot of well salted water to a boil. Add linguine and stir, Cook. Drain and set aside. Meanwhile, while pasta is cooking, heat olive oil in a large skillet or Dutch oven. Add raw garlic, shallots and sauté until shallots are transparent but not browned. Add crushed red pepper and marjoram, sauté for an additional 30 seconds. Increase heat.
Add white wine, bring to a boil and simmer until wine is reduced to 1/4 cup. Stir in undrained tomatoes and squeeze in roasted garlic.

Reduce heat and cook for 15 minutes. Add cooked linguine to pan and toss well to coat.

Turn off heat.

Add lemon juice, butter, basil and freshly ground pepper. Toss until well combined.

Garnish with lemon zest. Gremolata from the above recipe is also an excellent garnish for this dish.

Prep Time: 10 minutes (if garlic is roasted in advance, 50 if not)
Cook Time: 20 minutes
Total Time: 30 minutes or 1 hour 20 minutes
Yield: 4-6 servings
Difficulty Level: Easy

How To Roast Garlic

You'll Need:
2 heads garlic
2 tablespoons olive oil, or more to taste
Squares of aluminum foil torn to fit garlic

Directions:
Preheat oven to 425° F.
Slice off the very top of the garlic head, exposing tops of cloves.
 Place on a piece of foil and drizzle olive oil inside the head of garlic and using your hands, rub some on the outside.
Wrap tightly with foil and place on a cookie sheet and bake until tender and fragrant, about 45 minutes.
Remove from the oven and let cool until cool enough to handle.
 Peel outside skin off of bulbs and gently squeeze out cloves.
This can be done well in advance & stored in the fridge in a glass jar, covered with olive oil. Just squeeze the cloves into a jar and cover with olive oil to seal out air.It will easily keep a week or more if covered completely with oil & refrigerated.

 Prep Time: 5 minutes
Cook Time: 45 minutes
 Difficulty Level: Easy

How to Chiffonade Basil & Other Greens

Cutting something into a chiffonade possibly sounds like a strange and mysterious technique but it's actually just cutting any leafy thing such as basil, kale, or spinach into thin strips.
Trying to cut individual leaves can be difficult to cut by themselves, but when you stack them, the task becomes much easier. Your knife actually has something to sink its teeth into.
Begin by pulling the basil leaves off the stem and stacking them neatly in a pile with the stem ends all facing in one direction. The height of your stack depends on the thickness of your leaves and the sharpness of your knife.
 Larger, sturdier leaves such as kale are probably best done individually, use your judgment. Starting at the side, roll up your leaves with your stems parallel to the roll. Using your sharpest knife, begin slicing the roll perpendicularly, creating fine, thin strips.
The tighter your roll, the easier it is to make your slices thin. That's it! That's how you cut something into chiffonade!

Ziti with Eggplant and Tomatoes

This is fast & easy! I like to add 1/4 cup dry red wine to the vegetables after sautéing. For an extra boost of flavor and nutrition, add 1 (10 ounce) package of thawed spinach when you add the capers and olives.

You'll Need:
1 pound penne pasta
2 tablespoons extra virgin olive oil
6 cloves garlic, minced
1 onion, cut in thin wedges
1 red or green bell pepper, cut in strips
2 eggplants, cut into 1" pieces
1/2 teaspoon crushed red pepper flakes
1/2 cup water 1 (15 ounce) can diced tomatoes, undrained
1 (14 ounce) can tomato sauce
3 tablespoons capers
1/2 cup Kalamata olives, pitted & sliced
2 tablespoons chopped fresh parsley
Kosher salt & freshly ground black pepper, to taste

Directions:
Bring a large pot of well salted water to a boil. Add penne and cook until al dente. Drain, set aside.
While pasta cooks, heat olive oil in a large skillet, add onion, pepper, eggplant and garlic, sauté until lightly browned.
Add crushed red pepper & cook 30 seconds.
Add water, tomatoes and tomato sauce, reduce heat, cover. Simmer for 20 to 25 minutes. Add capers and olives, cook, stirring occasionally for 10 to 15 minutes.
 Add penne, stir to blend well, cook until heated through.
Serve & Enjoy!

Prep Time: 10 minutes

Cook Time: 50 minutes
Total Time: 60 minutes
Yield: Serves 6
Difficulty: Easy

Penne with Mushroom Sauce

For a 5 star restaurant dish, add a couple splashes of dry wine to your pan after sautéing the mushrooms. Dry vermouth is an especially good choice.

You'll Need:
1 pound penne or other tubular pasta
3 tablespoons butter
3 tablespoons extra virgin olive oil
8 cloves garlic, minced
1 bunch scallions, sliced
6 cups assorted mushrooms (portabella, golden chanterelle, shiitake, cremini, oyster, porcini, etc.), trimmed & sliced
1/8 teaspoon crushed red pepper
1 bay leaf
1 teaspoon dried thyme
1/4 teaspoon Kosher salt
 freshly ground black pepper, to taste
2 tablespoons olive oil
1/2 (5 ounce) container fresh baby spinach, cut in chiffonade

Optional garnish: Parmigiano-Reggiano cheese or Nutritional yeast flakes

Directions:
Bring a large pot of well salted water to a boil. Add penne.
Meanwhile: In large skillet or Dutch oven, heat 2 tablespoons butter and 1 tablespoon olive oil. Add scallions, and garlic, allow to brown slightly.
 Add, mushrooms, bay leaf. thyme, salt and pepper.
Cook, stirring occasionally, until mushrooms are just tender.
Add remaining butter and olive oil.
Stir and remove from heat. When penne is cooked (10-12 minutes), reheat the sauce and add parsley.

Mix with penne and enjoy.
Serve with a side of freshly sliced tomatoes.

Prep Time: 15 minutes
Cook Time: 15 minutes
Total Time: 30 minutes
Yield: 4-6 servings
Difficulty: Easy

Marinara Sauce

To me, there isn't another Marinara Sauce recipe that compares to the one belonging to the great team of Craig Claiborne and Pierre Franey. Always use a good quality, imported tomato such as San Marzano and great extra virgin olive oil and you'll have a winner every time! The only way I ever alter this recipe is to occasionally add 1/4 cup of good quality red or white wine to the pan after cooking the garlic. It just doesn't get any better than this. This is their original recipe and it makes a very small amount. I strongly suggest doubling it or even quadrupling it and freezing some to have on hand for your next pizza!

You'll Need:
2 1/2 cups imported canned tomatoes, such as San Marzano
2 tablespoons olive oil
1 tablespoon finely minced garlic
1/4 cup tomato paste
1 teaspoon dried oregano
Salt, if desired
Freshly ground pepper
1/4 cup finely chopped parsley

Directions:
Put the tomatoes through a sieve or puree them in the container of a food processor or blender. Heat the oil in a saucepan and add the garlic.
Cook briefly without browning.
Add the tomatoes, tomato paste, oregano, salt and pepper to taste.
Bring to the boil and let simmer 20 minutes.
Stir in the parsley.

Yield: About 2 3/4 cups
Originally published with Food; Rolling in Dough By Craig Claiborne; Pierre Franey, January 3, 1982 source

Vegan Mushroom and Eggplant "Meatballs"

Here's an excellent recipe to pair with the yummy marinara sauce. Add a green salad and some garlic bread and say Mangia! This recipe does take more than 30 minutes to prepare but it's an excellent recipe to prepare in advance, portion into serving size packages and store in the freezer. They're great to have on hand for fast evening meals either in a pasta dish or used to make subs.

You'll Need:
1 eggplant (3/4-1 pound), finely chopped
1/2 red bell pepper, finely minced
6-8 baby bella or cremini mushrooms, finely diced
1/2 large onion, finely diced
6 cloves garlic, minced
4 tablespoons extra virgin olive oil, divided
1/3 cup water
1 tablespoon fresh parsley, minced
1 cup Italian seasoned breadcrumbs
1 teaspoon dried oregano
1/4 - 1/2 teaspoon salt
Freshly ground black pepper

Directions:
In a large sauté pan with lid, heat 2 tablespoons olive oil over medium heat.
Add onions and cook until transparent.
Add garlic and remaining vegetables.
Cover with lid and let cook for 3-5 minutes.
Add 1/3 cup water, cover and cook for 20-30 minutes. stirring every 5 minutes or so.
After mixture has cooked about 30 minutes and is soft and thoroughly cooked through, add oregano, salt, pepper and fresh parsley.
Transfer eggplant, mushroom mixture to a bowl.

Add the bread crumbs a little at a time until all are incorporated.
Refrigerate for 30 minutes or more before proceeding with recipe.
Once the mixture has cooled, roll into approximately 18 meatballs or shape into patties .
Heat remaining olive oil in a sauté pan and lightly pan fry until browned.
Alternately, they can be baked at 375 F. but they'll be more moist if pan fried.
This recipe is easily multiplied and freezes well.

Prep Time: 15 minutes
Cook Time: (including refrigeration) 1 hour
Total Time: 1 hour 15 minutes
Yield: 4-6 servings Difficulty: Easy

3 Asian Inspired Pasta Dishes

Hoisin Noodles

I LOVE Hoisin Sauce. I love it's deep, dark, mysterious flavor so much I'll happily eat it right out of the jar with a spoon. I'm always looking for new and different ways to use it.
This dish is very easy to make and you can throw in whatever vegetables appeal to you.

You'll Need:
1 package rice noodles or 8 ounces buckwheat soba, vermicelli or angel hair pasta, cooked according to package instructions
1 tablespoon vegetable oil
1 (1 pound) package firm or extra firm tofu, drained and cut into 1/2" squares
3 cloves garlic, minced
3 cups mushrooms, sliced
2 carrots, peeled & sliced
1 red bell pepper. seeded & sliced into thin strips
4 cups Napa cabbage, chiffonade
1 heaping teaspoon fresh ginger, peeled & minced
1 10-ounce package frozen shelled Edamame, (about 2 cups), thawed
1 cup vegetable stock
1/3 cup Hoisin sauce
1 teaspoon Sriracha sauce or chili-garlic paste
1 teaspoon toasted sesame oil
1 tablespoon cornstarch
2 tablespoons cold water
2 cups mung bean sprouts
2 scallions, chopped

Directions:

Soak rice noodles, covered with hot water, 5-15 minutes, or until they're soft enough to eat, but still firm.
Drain & briefly rinse noodles with cold water to prevent sticking.
Set aside. OR cook buckwheat soba, vermicelli or angel hair pasta according to package directions. Drain & set aside.
In a large skillet, Dutch oven or wok, heat vegetable oil.
Add tofu, garlic, mushrooms and carrots.
Stir fry for about 4 minutes.
Add red bell pepper strips and Napa cabbage.
Cook and stir fry for an additional 4 minutes.
Add ginger and stir around in pan to combine for 30 seconds.
Add Edamame beans, and stock. Cook for 2 minutes more.
Add Hoisin sauce, Sriracha sauce, sesame oil, and stir to combine.
Combine cornstarch with cold water in a small dish.
Stir well.
Push vegetables to the side, making a well in center of pan, pour in cornstarch mixture & stir to blend.
Mixture is done when sauce turns almost clear.
Add mung bean sprouts, scallions & noodles.
Toss mixture together until heated through.
Serve & Enjoy!

Prep Time: 15 minutes
Cook Time: 20 minutes
Total Time: 35 minutes
Yield: 4 servings
Difficulty: Easy

Super Easy Asian Noodles

This isn't an authentic Asian pasta dish but it's FAST, EASY and DELICIOUS! Feel free to substitute whatever vegetables you have on hand. I like to add cut baby corn. You can also add small chunks of tofu to the pan when adding garlic.

You'll Need:
8 ounces spaghetti
2 teaspoon vegetable oil
2 cloves garlic, minced
1 small onion, sliced
1/4 cup green bell pepper, chopped
3 cups fresh broccoli, cut into florets
3/4 cup water
1/4 cup roasted peanuts, chopped
1/4 cup BB-Q sauce
1 tablespoon peanut butter, creamy
1 teaspoon soy sauce
1 teaspoon chili powder

Directions:
Cook spaghetti according to package directions and drain.
 While the pasta cooks: Heat a large nonstick skillet over medium-high heat.
Add oil and sauté garlic, onion and pepper until golden, about 3 minutes.
Add the water and the broccoli and cook until broccoli is tender-crisp, about 3 minutes.
Add cooked spaghetti and remaining ingredients.
Toss to coat until heated through.

Prep Time: 20 minutes
Cook Time: 6 minutes
Total time: 26 minutes

Yield: 4 servings
Difficulty Level: Super Easy

Asian Style Noodles With Tofu & Vegetables

You'll Need:
1 (16 ounce) package firm or extra firm tofu, drained & cut into 3/4" cubes
1/3 cup fat free Italian salad dressing
8 ounces uncooked angel hair pasta
1/4 cup vegetable broth
2 tablespoons minced fresh cilantro
2 tablespoons chunky peanut butter
1 tablespoon low sodium soy sauce
1 tablespoon agave nectar, honey, or other sweetener
1 teaspoon fresh ginger root, minced
1/2 teaspoon crushed red pepper
2 teaspoons toasted sesame oil
1/2 cups carrots, coarsely grated
1 medium onion, cut in thin wedges through root end.
1 cup fresh broccoli, cut in small florets
1 (6 ounce) package fresh pea pods, cut in julienne lengthwise
1/2 red bell pepper, cut in thin strips lengthwise
2 tablespoons canola oil
Finely chopped scallions for garnish

Directions:
In a large resealable zip top plastic bag, combine tofu and salad dressing. Seal bag, squeezing lightly to combine ingredients. Refrigerate for at least 15 minutes.
Meanwhile, cook pasta according to package directions.
Combine broth, cilantro, peanut butter, honey, soy sauce, ginger, sesame oil, set aside.
Heat canola oil in large sauté pan or wok.
Add crushed red pepper and swirl for 15 seconds.
Add carrots, onions. broccoli and pea pods, sauté for 3-5 minutes or until tender crisp.

Drain tofu, discarding marinade.
Add tofu to vegetables, cook for 2-3 minutes or until heated through.
Drain pasta and place in a large bowl.
Add tofu-veggie mixture and peanut butter mixture; toss to coat.
Garnish with chopped scallions

. Prep Time: 15 minutes
Cook Time: 15 minutes
Total Time: 30 minutes
Yield: 6 servings.
Difficulty: Easy

Note: If you have a peanut allergy, substitute tahini for the peanut butter. You'll probably want to increase the sweetener to taste as tahini is not as sweet as peanut butter.

Printed in Great Britain
by Amazon